A Family History

Tamiko

Tamiko Shimoyama
with Masako Glushien

Lulu Publishing Services rev. date: 5/28/2014

CONTENTS

Introduction

This book is based on a short memoir that my mother, Tamiko, handwrote on notepaper when she lived with my family—two young children (four and eight years old at the time), my husband, and me—in the US for fifteen months in 1988. It was her third visit; she stayed with us for a total of two years and nine months over her three visits. Having heard about her hard life, I suggested she write about it while she was with us.

I never saw her writing it. She wrote in the basement, a large, empty room that held only a television set and an old couch, where she felt comfortable recalling sometimes-painful memories. She removed a cushion from the couch and, sitting on the floor, Japanese style, used the wooden surface underneath as her makeshift desk. She wrote until my younger child came home from school and then spent time with her upstairs.

When she was at the final writing stage, she cut out small strips from white stickers to cover her mistakes and make corrections, showing her painstaking effort to write correctly. She never showed it to me until she finished, when she asked me to make a cover for the fifteen pages of her memoir.

Preoccupied with raising my children, I didn't read it until twenty years later. I sent a copy to my oldest brother, who was living in Japan. He typed copies from her handwritten memoir for our siblings and relatives, but when he read the chapter about Tamiko's mother's death, he was moved to tears and had to stop typing for a while. It was at that time that my mother's life changed drastically and she began to face a chain of hardships.

My mother's life journey was both remarkable and poignant. When she was a teenager, there was neither local public transportation nor electricity; she walked wherever she needed to go and washed clothes in the icy-cold river without soap.

My father's life as a child was very different from my mother's. He grew up in a wealthy family with live-in servants who called him "Botchan," which means "young master." As an adult, he was kind and well-liked and constantly innovated new ways to make ends meet, but few of his plans ever came to fruition. As a result of business failures, my parents struggled to raise their five children.

I appreciated my mother's effort to write down her life journey, and I want to share the stories about her life. I filled in some missing stories by means of phone conversations with her from Japan.

I took great care in translation. I restudied English grammar and writing, attended private writing classes, and received grammar advice from friends and endless help and support from my two adult children, my son-in-law, and my husband. I wanted to ensure that my mother's stories reflected her experiences in living through many changes in Japanese society, from male chauvinism to rapidly evolving technology to the country's emergence as a global economic power.

I am happy to tell the stories of the foundation of Tamiko's family and her experience of seeing her brother's miraculous recovery, which became a pillar of her faith in God. This is what gave her the strength to overcome the many hardships in her life, which inspired me to live my life with faith and determination and to teach my children to do the same.

Masako Glushien

Tamiko's Early Life

Tamiko Ichimoto was born on July 28, 1917, in Okuhata, a small village in Yamaguchi prefecture that is next to Hiroshima, Japan. She was the second of six children. The house where she grew up stood on a stone foundation at the foot of a low mountain overlooking a rice field. There were also a small shrine and a courtyard in the distance where she made a shortcut to her school.

Tamiko's father in his 50s.

Tamiko's father, Hiroyuki Ichimoto, was a farmer who later became a minister of Tenri-kyo, one of the Shinto religions in Japan. Her mother, Ikuyo Hanata Ichimoto, was a skilled seamstress who taught sewing to many of the villagers. When Ikuyo was a child, her parents were recruited by the prefectural government to work as pioneers in Hawaii, growing coffee beans on land that was offered to them. They sent money home so Ikuyo and her younger brother could have the best education and living standards while their grandparents raised them. Ikuyo's parents returned to Japan many years later with sufficient money to remodel their house for comfortable living.

Tamiko's paternal grandfather, Chujiro Ichimoto, held a high position in the county government and taught at the private elementary school in his spare time. One day the area where he worked suffered a severe flood, and despite the danger, he worked in the water for many hours to save as many of the county office's valuable documents and items as he could. That evening he was rushed to the hospital, suffering from exhaustion. He developed pneumonia and died at the age of twenty-seven, never having returned home.

It was the second major flood incident in the same area, and many people died. A large roadside monument was placed as a dedication to all the flood victims. To prevent more flooding, the prefecture began building Yashiro Dam in 1974 and completed it in 1991.

Hiroyuki was only two years old when his father died. A year after Chujiro's death, Hiroyuki's mother, Shitsu, remarried and moved away, leaving Hiroyuki with Chujiro's parents. She often tried to see him while he was a child, but Chujiro's parents discouraged her from seeing him and painted her as a bad person because she left him behind when she remarried. However, Hiroyuki was the only heir, and in those days the heir could not go anywhere, even if Shitsu wanted to raise him elsewhere. Therefore, if she had to follow her new husband, she could not take Hiroyuki with her. It was unfortunate that Hiroyuki never made any effort to establish a relationship with his mother, which affected his entire life and meant that Tamiko would never know much about Shitsu, her grandmother.

Entering Yashiro Elementary School

When Tamiko was seven, Ikuyo took her to the school's opening ceremony. Tamiko was dressed in a beautiful kimono Ikuyo had made and carried the school bag Ikuyo had embroidered with spring flowers and butterflies. Everyone admired the outfit and Ikuyo's ability to make everything so pretty.

Tamiko enjoyed going to school, even though it took twenty-five minutes to walk there. The school was a one-room schoolhouse that sixteen students between the first and fourth grades from six villages in her town attended.

During the Taisho Emperor era, the students were taught that the emperor was a living god, and they lived in a male-chauvinistic society. Therefore, it did not matter whether Tamiko achieved high marks in school, as only boys were chosen to be class leaders.

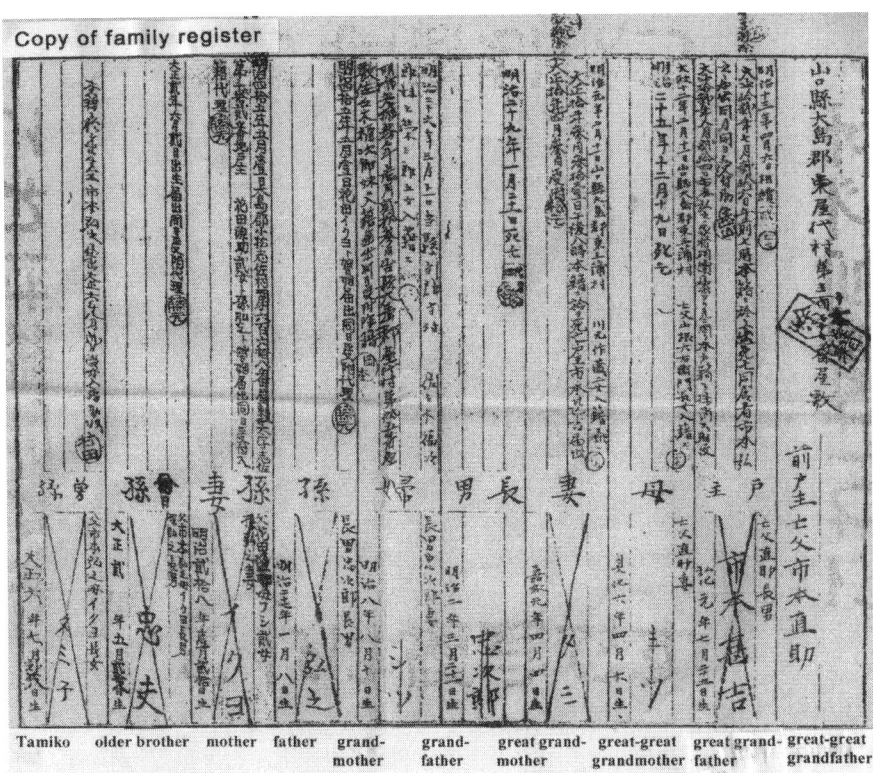

Copy of family register

Tamiko	older brother	mother	father	grand-mother	grand-father	great grand-mother	great-great grandmother	great grand-father	great-great grandfather

Above: One of the official copies of Tamiko's family register that recorded five generations.

Left: This stone monument was placed in 1889, in memory of the 110 victims from the flood of 1886.

Ten years later, the great flood occurred at the same place where Tamiko's grandfather worked, and he became one of the flood victims.

(Photographed by Tamiko's niece Eiko)

The only teacher, Mr. Mori, began the last class of each day by writing quizzes on the blackboard, and each student was dismissed as soon as he or she finished the quizzes correctly. Tamiko excelled in academics, and she was always the first one to be dismissed. She was proud that she always went home first. Since no one else had been dismissed, she walked home alone, and on the way home classmates' parents often asked her, "Why isn't my kid with you?"

Tamiko was a tomboy as a child, and she loved to climb trees. There weren't many other girls playing outside, as they were busy doing house chores instead. When Ikuyo asked Tamiko to watch her younger sister, Mitsue, Tamiko often gave the chore to another sister, Fujiko, to do, so she could spend more time outdoors playing. Ikuyo eventually gave up asking her to help, but she was pleased that Tamiko always brought home good grades from school.

When Tamiko was in the fourth grade, the schoolgirls had to add a home economics class, such as sewing. Ikuyo had taught Tamiko's sewing teacher how to sew, so it was a strange situation.

Tamiko's sister, Mitsue (nine years younger), in her sewing class. When Tamiko was in fourth grade, everyone wore a kimono like the teacher (right). This photo shows the remarkable changes in clothing and increasing class size over the years, circa 1936.

(Photo courtesy of Tamiko's nephew Masanori)

A Guardian Angel

Once the students reached the fifth grade, they had to go to a bigger school that was farther away, and it took Tamiko about an hour to walk there.

One afternoon in May, Tamiko, who was eleven years old at the time, and her friend Takeko were caught in a rainstorm on the way home from school. When they reached a narrow bridge that had no railings, they were afraid to cross. Despite strong winds, Tamiko began crossing first, holding a closed umbrella under her arm. When she was halfway across the bridge, the gusty wind suddenly opened her umbrella and threw her into the raging, muddy stream below. She struggled to hold on to a rock as the rushing water swallowed her umbrella. She was terrified, and she knew she was going down next. Takeko was terrified by the frightening scene but courageously ran across the bridge and, crying all the way to Tamiko's home, told Ikuyo what had happened.

Sometime after Takeko left, Tamiko passed out from exhaustion. When she regained consciousness, she found herself between two large rocks near the riverbank. She didn't know how she had come to be there. She grabbed the tall grass on the bank and crawled onto a rock.

Miraculously, Ikuyo found her and pulled her to safety. Ikuyo was barefoot, having run out of the house without stopping to put on shoes when she heard what had happened. Ikuyo didn't care that she and Tamiko were soaked by the heavy rain, and she was happy carrying Tamiko home on her back, telling her how she learned about the incident from the trembling Takeko, who thought Tamiko had been swept away. Takeko was waiting with Tamiko's younger siblings when they returned home.

Tamiko realized that she must have struggled in the raging water for at least thirty minutes, as it would have taken that much time for Takeko to notify Ikuyo and for Ikuyo to run back to the river. Takeko was in tears but rejoiced when she saw that Tamiko was safe. When

Hiroyuki arrived home, he was deeply relieved to see his daughter was alive, but he couldn't figure out how such a little girl could have survived without any physical harm. He felt certain that it was the help of a guardian angel.

Perhaps she was spared because a year later her family would need her badly.

After that nightmarish event, Tamiko took the longer way home to avoid crossing that bridge. She could not bear to see the fast current of the river again.

In the years around 1929, compulsory education in Japan ended in the sixth grade, but Ikuyo wanted Tamiko to pursue secondary education. She consulted with Tamiko's teacher, Ms. Murata, who agreed to help Tamiko prepare for the difficult entrance examination to enter today's seventh grade. Tamiko often stayed at school until sundown, studying for the exam.

The Japanese educational system was reformed in 1947, extending compulsory education to ninth grade. All students in Japan still today must take an entrance examination to qualify for senior high school (grades ten through twelve) and undergraduate school.

Around this time, indoor lighting moved from oil lamps to electric lights, but the roads from school to Tamiko's home were still dark. No one unfamiliar with the area could have found Tamiko's street without knowing the way. Tamiko hated going home in the dark. She calculated which way was the shortest and ran through the forest in the shrine courtyard with the help of the moonlight. Ikuyo waited anxiously for her each evening and sighed deeply each time she walked in, saying, "Oh, thank God you are home safely."

Tamiko was one of three students, and the only girl, in her class of forty-five who prepared to pursue higher education. Ms. Murata was the best teacher around, and because of her help, Tamiko was well-prepared for the test and waited with confidence for the test day.

The Death of Mother

When Tamiko was twelve years old, her maternal grandfather's first-year memorial service was scheduled for March 14, and her family was getting ready to gather at her grandmother's house.

In the morning, Ikuyo dressed Tamiko and her older brother, Tadao, in new kimonos she had made. She was very pleased with how both of them looked. She sent Tadao to the altar with some offerings and told him that the rest of the family would catch up soon. Tamiko stayed behind to help Ikuyo get ready.

As soon as Tadao left, Ikuyo said, "I don't feel well. I need to lie down for a little while." Tamiko was troubled at first, but she believed Ikuyo would be well soon. That afternoon, Hiroyuki decided to fetch the doctor. It took him an hour to get to the doctor's office on foot and another hour to return with the doctor. Tamiko felt that two hours was awfully long for her mother to wait, but nothing else could be done, and finally Ikuyo received medical treatment. Everyone believed that she was getting better, and the family dozed off on the floor at her bedside.

At about ten o'clock that night, Tamiko opened her eyes, and Hiroyuki said, "Your mother died." She thought she was having a bad dream until he said again, "Mother died." Tamiko screamed, "You are lying! I don't believe you!" Hiroyuki also wished it had been a lie.

Someone had to tell Tamiko's grandmother, her uncle, and her older brother, who had waited long hours at her grandmother's house for the family to arrive. How could they bear such bad news? They had all looked forward to getting together on this day, but not for her mother's death. Finally, one of her neighbors brought the sad message to Tamiko's grandmother. No one could believe that Ikuyo, having seemed well in the morning, was gone the same night. After all, she had never been ill before. Ikuyo died from meningitis at the age of thirty-five, leaving behind her husband and six children between the ages of one and sixteen. Fortunately, none of the other family members became ill with it. How could the family sustain their lives and move on? It seemed that everything had ended.

The next day, Tamiko's grandmother quickly finished the memorial service for her husband and came with Tamiko's uncle and her older brother to join the family to prepare for Ikuyo's funeral. The family was stricken with disbelief and terrible sadness.

After the funeral service, as Ikuyo's body was leaving their house for the cemetery, Tamiko cried and screamed, "Wait! I am going in the coffin! She is alone in there! I am staying with my mother. She is not ready to leave us. She can't go yet!" Everyone cried as they watched the distraught Tamiko. Her younger siblings were too young to understand what death meant, but they were crying as well. Tamiko was confused with grief. After Ikuyo's burial, the visitors returned to the house and then left the family one by one. Tamiko finally realized that her mother was not coming back.

Good-Bye to School

Ms. Murata, who had prepared Tamiko for the entrance test, asked Hiroyuki how Tamiko was going to pursue her education. Hiroyuki knew that Tamiko wanted to go to school, but although she, Hiroyuki, and Tamiko exchanged no words, all of them understood. Who else could care for her baby brother? It was clear that continuing her schooling was impossible. Tamiko tearfully said good-bye to her teacher and to school as well. It all seemed so unfair because her older brother could stay at school. In those days, males rarely did any domestic chores; instead, they were expected to be the breadwinners.

The kimono in which Ikuyo had dressed Tamiko before she died was the last gift from her mother. Tamiko lost all hope and didn't know how to dig herself out of her situation. Hiroyuki said sadly, "If this baby hadn't been born, you wouldn't have such a hard life." Everyone cried because they had lost the person who was the most precious to them. They wanted only Ikuyo, who was like the sun to them.

Caring for the Baby Brother, Saburo

At the age of twelve, Tamiko suddenly faced the reality of not having her mother around and quickly had to figure out how to do all the house chores.

Without milk for her baby brother, Saburo, she had to soak and grind mochi rice into milk, then warm it up, being careful not to let it turn into a sticky, undrinkable form. Making milk was an exhausting chore, but Saburo couldn't have solid food yet. He was always hungry, and every time he cried, she cried too. He lost weight and was growing poorly. He was vulnerable to catching colds and suffered from bedsores, so Tamiko had to carry him on her back day and night and take him to the doctor nearly every day.

She was embarrassed to be carrying Saburo on her back when she bumped into her old schoolmates during the one-hour walk to the doctor's office. When Tamiko recognized someone she knew in the distance, she walked a longer route to avoid being seen. The shame she felt became a burden, as her classmates believed she was in school.

Only housework waited for her at home. Every day she went to the creek to do the laundry while carrying Saburo on her back. If there was a stain on a piece of clothing, she had to pat it on a stone with a wooden stick to get it out. Although there was soap, it had such a harsh odor that Hiroyuki used it only to wash his ox.

She couldn't put Saburo down because of his bedsores, so she often fell asleep in a sitting position with him still on her back. Two other young siblings, ages three and five, were also waiting to be cared for. Her eight-year-old sister helped with the household chores if she wasn't busy with her schooling.

Many challenges lay ahead; in the hot summer Tamiko couldn't store many vegetables, so she had to cook them for meals based on how quickly they would spoil. In the winter she dug a hole in the mud under the removable floorboards in the dining room; laid down hay; placed raw vegetables like potatoes, sweet potatoes, lotus, and burdock roots on the hay; and then covered them with more hay. She pickled other vegetables, such as eggplant, cabbage, and cucumber, in salt, but even they didn't last long. She washed, peeled, and hung out to dry fruits like persimmons to be eaten as dessert. She heated bathing water on the fire and saved the ashes to be used as fertilizer for the garden or to help wash dishes. Getting water was also troublesome, as it had to be collected by the bucketful from a big water bin made of clay in the yard, where water flowed from a nearby mountain stream and drained out from a bamboo pipe.

With little to comfort her, Tamiko often visited her mother's grave and cried, "I want to go with Saburo to where you are." She sought relief, but it was hopeless. She went home, her eyes swollen with weeping. With her life flipped upside down, she was no longer herself and didn't know if she could persevere. There seemed to be no solution.

Saburo Becomes Blind

Warm weather finally arrived at the end of June. Hiroyuki taught Tamiko's two younger siblings to look after themselves and to do some light chores when Tamiko needed to leave the house to take care of other chores. They usually played at neighbors' houses during the day.

Tamiko often had to take Saburo to see the doctor, who advised her to watch over him because he might catch measles. (Vaccinations for measles would not be available until thirty years later.) While Tamiko's other siblings had already had measles, Saburo was weak and Hiroyuki worried about whether he could survive it.

One day, Saburo had a high fever, and three days later a bright red rash appeared. By the fourth and fifth day, the rash had spread all over his body. When Hiroyuki said, "The toughest days are over; he will get better soon," Tamiko was relieved.

The next day the rash had disappeared completely, but Saburo's eyes were glued shut, and he couldn't open them. Tamiko and Hiroyuki took him to the eye specialist, who told them that the measles virus had attacked Saburo's eyes, which had been damaged from the high fever. The doctor treated him but said, "There is no way to save his eyes, even if he undergoes surgery when he gets older and stronger."

Tamiko walked home feeling hopeless, as if she were wearing a pair of iron shoes. She reported to her grandmother and to the church that Saburo would never see again.

Hiroyuki Makes a Pledge to God

Hiroyuki did not know what his own future held, but he was ready to do whatever he could do to help Saburo. He prayed, "Almighty God, please give me the strength and courage for Saburo, who is going through a terrible time in his life." He felt that his little son's blindness was a calling from God, and he made a pledge to serve God, even if there was to be no positive outcome for Saburo. Accepting Hiroyuki's pledge, the headmaster of the church guided Hiroyuki and Tamiko to join in prayers for three days and three nights.

The people who knew the family often asked where they went every day, and Tamiko's reply was, "We go to the church to pray for my brother's recovery." They ridiculed her, saying that the family had lost its mind and that it would be like flowers blossoming from roasted seeds if their prayer were answered. Tamiko ignored what other people thought.

Miracle

The third day after the family began praying at the church, Tamiko was cooking fish at home, carrying Saburo on her back as usual. Suddenly, Saburo said, "Fish, Fish!" She knew he was hungry and thought that he could tell what she was cooking by the smell. She put him down to feed him, but to her astonishment, his eyes were open, but they were red like a rabbit's eyes.

"You can see!" Tamiko exclaimed. She kneeled down and thanked God. Feeling humbled and ecstatic, she quickly put Saburo onto her back and rushed to tell Hiroyuki, who was working in his garden. She screamed, "Saburo opened his eyes, and he can see!"

Hiroyuki stopped working and looked closely at Saburo's eyes. Tears rolled down Hiroyuki's cheeks, and he and Tamiko kneeled down and cried with joy.

That day was the happiest day of Tamiko's life. She and Hiroyuki hurried home, had lunch, and then headed to the church with Saburo. There they expressed their gratitude, saying, "Thank you, God; you heard our prayers." They went to church every day to clean Saburo's eyes with the sacred water that was in the sanctuary of the shrine. Every time Tamiko wiped his eyes, thick, dark yellow mucus smeared onto gauze pads. A week later, his eyes began to clear. *Indeed*, Tamiko thought, *God exists*. She believed that Saburo's eyes were healed with the power of prayers.

A sick child, at age three Saburo still couldn't stand up on his own. Tamiko often wondered whether she would ever see him walk. Finally, two years after Ikuyo's death, he began walking. She was happy to show Saburo off to her neighbors, saying, "He is walking by himself!"

She understood that her survival from the rainstorm was, so she could help her family, but her teenage years went by quickly as she looked after four younger siblings.

Hiroyuki left his six children behind in Tamiko's care to attend a ministry school in Tenri City in Nara, Japan, where the Shinto church headquarters was located. With their father away, Tamiko was in charge of her four younger siblings and their care, and only her older brother, Tadao, knew her pain and anguish. Tadao eventually gave up going to college so he could work the farm and become the head of the household.

Mitsuji, age twenty-six:
Dressed in religious garb at
Tenri school in Nara, Japan.

Tamiko, age eighteen:
This outfit was a gift from her
uncle who lived in Hawaii.

Attending the Local Sewing Class

When Tamiko was sixteen, two years after Saburo started to play alone, Hiroyuki offered to let her attend sewing classes as an opportunity to "learn for her future." In those days young girls needed to know how to sew a kimono before marrying and leaving home.

It was a beautiful April day when the class started, and Tamiko took Saburo there every day during the first year. He never disturbed the class, and everyone was supportive. One teacher even offered to give Tamiko some sewing supplies and encouraged her to attend all classes. People who knew her offered sewing jobs, which helped to pay for her tuition. During her second year, a relative watched Saburo while Tamiko was in the class.

When Tamiko was eighteen, she completed the class and planned to pursue the advanced level, but Hiroyuki told her to go to Tenri City, Japan, to study religion.

It was the first time Tamiko left her hometown. While studying for six months at the school in Tenri City, she discovered a quiet and peaceful life. There, she became acquainted with her future husband, Mitsuji, who was born on March 6, 1909, and was eight years her senior. He was in the same dormitory and much older than many other students, so he became the dorm leader and was endearingly nicknamed "Grandpa."

Upon graduation in 1935, Mitsuji and Tamiko went back to their respective hometowns (about 250 miles apart), and did not correspond, so it seemed as though their friendship had ended. It was out of the question for Tamiko even to think of marrying him because a matchmaker or parents customarily made arrangements for marriage while considering social status, age, wealth, and education, among other criteria.

Outbreak of the War

In 1937 Mitsuji was deployed to China at the beginning of the Second Japan-China War. He was a reservist at the time, as all men were drafted at the age of twenty at that time. Within a few months of fighting in China, he was shot above his right knee. If it had not been for his injury, he might have been killed in action, as the war soon escalated into World War II. Mitsuji was admitted for treatment of his wounded leg at a temporary medical shelter outside of Japan.

Meanwhile, Tamiko was volunteering at her church, preparing care packages. Coincidentally, the packages she prepared were sent to the medical shelter where Mitsuji was being treated, and among the many care packages and wounded soldiers, one package with Tamiko's name found its way into Mitsuji's hands. Surprised by the improbable coincidence, Mitsuji thought it was like a twist of fate. Despite the uplifting experience, Mitsuji's condition deteriorated, as his wound became infected. Maggots were nesting inside his wound, which created excruciating pain. A doctor told him that amputation was imminent. When Mitsuji's parents were notified about the condition of his injured leg and the possibility of amputation, they were devastated. Feeling helpless, Mitsuji's mother began a hundred consecutive days of faithful prayers at the shrine on the mountain near their house. When Mitsuji returned to Japan for proper treatment, he avoided amputation and believed that his mother's prayers had played a significant part in that outcome.

Before his deployment to China, Mitsuji was briefly married by arrangement, but he was divorced while he focused on getting well. Following his recovery, he confessed to his father, who didn't know Tamiko, that he wanted to marry her. As Mitsuji had been nearly killed in action, his father granted his wish and went to visit Tamiko and Hiroyuki in their hometown. They were surprised and happy, and Hiroyuki believed that they were well-suited to each other. Hioyuki decided to arrange their marriage through their mutual church contact.

Mitsuji in army uniform.

Cover photo:
Wearing Tamiko's self-made
kimono, age twenty-three:
This beautifully woven
handbag was crafted by
Mitsuji during his
hospitalization, and was
admired by many people.

Marriage

With Japan still at war, the scarcity of goods and supplies took a toll on Tamiko's wedding preparations. Hiroyuki couldn't buy her a wedding kimono, so she borrowed one that Mitsuji's older sisters had worn.

On May 23, 1940, Tamiko married Mitsuji Shimoyama at the Shimoyamas' residence in the countryside town of Shimokume, in Hyogo Prefecture, Japan, about forty-five miles north of Kobe City. Mitsuji's parents lived with them, as Mitsuji was the only son among six siblings and the heir of the family, so he was responsible for taking care of his parents in their old age. The family grew quickly, and by end of the war, Mitsuji and Tamiko had three children; the older son, Yoshimi; the second son, Yukio; and a daughter, Keiko.

During the war, everyone depended on rations and had to bear the hardship of food shortages. Farmers were ordered to surrender what they produced to the government, and everyone was hungry. If Tamiko was lucky, her neighbor would share food that was just enough to feed one person, but Tamiko also had to feed her parents-in-law and her three children. With fresh food in short supply, people often got sick from spoiled food.

Because of the shortage of electricity, electric service was suspended during the day, so they looked forward to listening to limited radio broadcasts in the evenings.

On August 6, 1945, an atomic bomb was dropped on Hiroshima, instantly killing between sixty and eighty thousand people and destroying the city. Even today, no one knows exactly how many people were killed on impact because so many documents were destroyed in the blast.

The news of the attack took nearly two days to reach Tamiko's town through the limited radio news broadcasts. The reports were vague, leaving many people confused about the nature of the attack.

One of Tamiko's sisters, who lived in the small town about fifty miles west of Hiroshima City, recalled seeing a small article in the newspaper the next day but dismissed it as just another bombing. Eventually, people started noticing that their neighbors who had gone to Hiroshima for work never returned. With no knowledge of the dangers involved, many volunteers in the rescue mission to Hiroshima were recruited from her town and suffered from a mysterious illness known today as radiation poisoning.

News of a second bomb in Nagasaki, combined with stories about victims who burned to ashes, created a sense of panic throughout Tamiko's town. Rumors spread fast in the countryside, with each new one adding another piece to the puzzle of the scope of destruction that had taken place. Some doctors began noticing that the survivors developed mysterious sicknesses, which they thought were infectious diseases, while another rumor spread that survivors were getting sick or dying from exposure to rainfall called "black rain." At the time, nobody had heard of an atomic bomb or radiation poisoning, but even those who lived far from the bombsite began worrying about rainfall that might carry something life-threatening.

Tamiko was perplexed about how the war could have become so inhumane. A longing for a peaceful life one day was in everyone's hearts.

The War in the Pacific Ends

Early on the morning of August 15, 1945, a notice was delivered to each house announcing that Emperor Hirohito would be giving a speech at noon. Everyone wondered what had happened, and all were glued to the radio broadcast at noon. It was the first time they had heard his voice, but because of the poor audio transmission, the message was not clear. However, everyone believed what the emperor had announced was that Japan had been defeated and the war had ended.

Everyone had believed that they were going to win the war, which was why they had sacrificed almost everything. After all that they had endured, the truth was crushing. They were afraid of what defeat would mean and what was going to happen next. Would the American army invade their lives? Anxiety and fear occupied everyone's minds.

There were many rumors, and Tamiko's family and friends discussed where they could hide once the American soldiers entered their area, which seemed to be imminent. Perhaps they needed to dig trenches or hide in the woods.

After many anxious days had passed, there were new rumors that there was ample food in the city because the US's occupation forces had brought food and necessities. They began to feel more positive that there was hope that they could rebuild their lives. Everyone began to smile more often. Months passed, and finally their lives started to improve.

A few years later, buoyed by a little financial stability, Tamiko and Mitsuji had two more children; their third son, Kaoru, and their second daughter, Masako.

Mitsuji's parents:
Mitsu (left) and Chutaro, circa 1940s.

*Mitsuji and Tamiko were married at the Shimoyamas' house
on May 23, 1940.*

Front view of the Shimoyamas' house.

Back view of the house surrounded by rice fields.

The First Business in the City of Kobe

Mitsuji's leg injury from the war made farm work difficult, and he knew he couldn't continue to support his family as a farmer. Seeking new job opportunities, he decided to visit the city of Kobe. He packed two bags of rice in his backpack to barter for something useful and traveled to the city. When he arrived, he could not believe his eyes, as he had not imagined the magnitude of destruction to the city from the war.

At the time, rice was a restricted commodity in the city, and each household was limited to a monthly ration with strict purchase regulations. In addition to each household's purchase records being kept in a rice passbook, there were also rumors of police guarding the railways, as rice was sometimes considered more valuable than land. No one understood how Mitsuji had managed to bring rice into the city in defiance of the rules.

Walking around in an area that had once prospered, Mitsuji happened to pass by a landowner who stopped him and asked what was in his bag. Happy to find rice, the landowner asked to exchange the rice for the right to lease his plot of land. The land was in front of a well-known shrine and near the Kobe station, and Mitsuji sensed it would be a good deal in the long run, so he made an agreement to hand over 2-hyos of rice (hyo is an old Japanese counter for a cylindrical bag that was woven by straw to contain about 132 lbs of rice) when Mitsuji returned to the plot with wood to build his store.

Mitsuji hurried to gather building materials, primarily wood cut from trees on the mountain that was part of his land. When Mitsuji returned to his property with a truck filled with wood and five carpenters, he was surprised to discover that other construction had begun to encroach onto his property. (Without the proper law and order in postwar Japan, many ownership disputes were settled on a build-first basis.) After he reclaimed his right to build on his land, Mitsuji built his store. Many other stores and houses were built, and some large buildings, including a Kabuki theater, a courthouse, and Mitsukoshi

Department Store, were renovated at their original locations in the neighborhood.

Mitsuji's first business in the city was an ice cream shop, which he ran in the spring and summer and converted into a teahouse in the fall and winter. Always packed with customers, the store received large orders of coffee and tea every day from the theater, the department store, and the courthouse. The business was a success from the start, and Mitsuji soon hired six employees.

Although Mitsuji had many innovative ideas, he often surrendered to the many obstacles in business and jumped to a new idea. The cutthroat business world seemed to sense his weakness and take advantage of him, which led many of his businesses to fail.

As the heir in his family, he had the responsibility of caring for his parents in their old age, so he commuted to their house in the countryside every ten days. When he returned to the shop one day, he realized that something was wrong. After paying the expenses, there was no money left, yet the business had many customers. Suspecting his employees were embezzling, he decided to stay in the city as long as possible. Sadly, his mother passed away around this time.

After one of his trips, he came back unannounced and caught his employees hiding cash in their apron pockets instead of depositing it in the store's cash box. Since he could not depend on his employees, Mitsuji and Tamiko made the difficult decision to move their family of eight—three adults, including Mitsuji's father, and five children between two and nine years old—to the city. There were many challenges to living in a big city, but it seemed to be the only way to secure their future.

The Family Moves to Kobe City

The family arrived in Kobe City on the afternoon of April 1, 1950, and soon were busy settling in. The five-year-old daughter, Keiko, who was curious about her surroundings, was especially intrigued by the sight of the streetcar, and she hoped to ride on it someday. Early that evening, Keiko was playing by herself on the iron railing in front of the neighborhood store when a policeman asked her, "Where are you from? Where are your parents?" She said nothing but pointed to the streetcar. The policeman asked, "Where is your house?" Keiko said, "I don't know, but I remember the house is in front of the shrine." The kind policeman put her on a streetcar to find a shrine that she might recognize.

When it was too dark to see outside, the policeman finally gave up on the search and took her back to the police station to check the missing-person reports before contacting the staff at a nearby orphanage. Orphans and homeless people were common in the neighborhood, so a member of the staff came to pick up Keiko, and they began walking toward the shelter. Suddenly Keiko saw the shrine and cried, "This one! This one!" The staff member went to each house near the shrine until he found the right one. Keiko probably would have noticed the shrine much earlier because she was already in the right neighborhood, but when the policeman suggested riding the streetcar to find her house, she became too distracted with her adventure to think about going home.

The next day, Mitsuji and Tamiko were ordered to the police station, where they were reprimanded and told that, if they failed to be more attentive to their younger children, they would face a serious charge. They apologized deeply and were embarrassed for not even realizing that Keiko had been missing. They had wanted to send her to a day-care center near their house but were told that it was full. Thanks to the policeman's intervention, the principal of the center was persuaded to accept her.

When the family began their new life in the city, the oldest son, Yoshimi, was entering third grade, and the middle son, Yukio, was going into first grade. The boys would have to adjust to a new school and make new friends. Tamiko and Mitsuji were anxious about sending their children to a school in the big city, and Mitsuji's father, who was eighty-one, had trouble adjusting to the new place. Sadly, he died six months later.

One afternoon, Yoshimi didn't come home from school at the usual time. He had a country accent, and about ten classmates had ambushed him on the way home. They often yelled at him, "You are a fresh kid. A country kid should stay behind us!" They wanted to teach him a lesson so he would stay behind them in academics. Luckily, Yoshimi was a fast runner.

When Mitsuji looked for him, Yoshimi was hiding behind a large rock in the woods of the shrine courtyard in front of their house. Mitsuji called, "You are safe now! I'm here to protect you! Come out!" Yoshimi came out cautiously. He had lost his shoes, and his feet were covered in blood from running barefoot, but he didn't cry. He was determined to be strong against the bullies.

Yoshimi went back to school the next day with his father. Mitsuji said to his classmates, "I'm not here to punish anyone who ambushed my son yesterday, but if you did and you are brave enough, raise your hand." Surprisingly, some of the bullies raised their hands! Then Mitsuji said, "I'm going to tell you about my son. He was a smart student in the country school too, but his old classmates never hurt him. It is a shame to feel that he is a threat to you or to feel insulted by him. Let's try to be good to each other. Then something good will come out of it." Over the next few days, Mitsuji went to school with Yoshimi, and the harassment against him stopped.

While the business had flourished, Mitsuji began to face a string of obstacles. Other businesses began copying his business, and gangsters started harassing and threatening his employees for money. Customers stopped coming in because of the gangster's presence.

Law and order were all but absent. Overwhelmed by these challenges, Mitsuji closed his first business. While Tamiko worried about how they would feed their children, Mitsuji remained optimistic and assured her, "I will come up with a new business soon. Don't worry."

Mitsuji Opens a Pachinko Parlor

Needing a new business, Mitsuji decided to open a pachinko parlor. Pachinko is a Japanese gambling machine that is a cross between a pinball machine and a slot machine. Being the first in the district, it was an immediate success and a ray of sunshine in the area. Unfortunately, it did not last long, as larger stores began opening parlors in the vicinity with more attractive rewards and quickly drew most of his customers away. Mitsuji closed his business again.

Around this time, many homeless people who had lost everything from the war were living around the shrine, so the shrine's courtyard became a place filled with many characters.

One cold winter day, the family saw a man called "the garlic man," who attracted large audiences in the courtyard. He exclaimed, "When you eat lots of garlic, you won't feel cold, so I'm going to demonstrate to prove that!" Then he submerged himself in a metal drum filled with cold water. Nobody knew what the garlic man's real profession was, but he was homeless. A few days later, Mitsuji invited the man to stay at his house, but the man ate so much garlic every day that the smell became intolerable, and Tamiko and their children began complaining. Mitsuji felt for the garlic man but had to ask him to leave.

At that time Japan was still suffering economic distress from the war, despite being under the auspices of the American government. Mitsuji found it increasingly difficult to continue his business in competition with large companies, and the family had to live off the money from selling some of his assets in the countryside.

Eventually, Mitsuji rented a small store in the neighborhood shopping mall and began selling daily commodities. This also ended in failure, so he started a snack store the following summer. Sadly, someone falsely accused his employee of being sick with cholera, and the health department forced him to close the shop, although they had no proof. Again, he had to think of another business.

Tamiko felt hopeless from the constant financial hardships but remained strong for their five young children. She believed in Mitsuji, who had so often come up with new business ideas, and hoped better days would soon come.

Center: This is the original store and house in the back when Tamiko's family moved to the city. The mochi store ended in failure here. This store was also used for an election campaign, enabling Mitsuji to achieve economic stability.

Rising Again

In the fall of 1951 Mitsuji opened a Japanese delicacy store that sold snacks made from mochi rice, which is pounded into a sticky paste and formed into rice cakes. He employed two craftsmen and four store associates, and the store was an astonishing success, with people lining up around the block to buy the beautiful delicacies as quickly as they were displayed. The workers woke up at two in the morning and worked into the evening every day, and the store became well-known in the neighborhood.

One day, when everyone was preoccupied with the store, Tamiko and Mitsuji thought their youngest child, Masako, who was about four years old, was playing by the side of the store. When they discovered she was missing, everyone panicked, but before reporting it to the police, Mitsuji rushed to see if she had somehow gone home alone and found her three houses down from their house, playing with her friend.

Masako showed Mitsuji the path she took from the store, and he was amazed that it was the exact way he rode from their home to the store on his bike, even though he had done the ride with her only a few times. The family slept at the shop many nights. It took Tamiko at least fifteen minutes to walk home and should have taken Masako at least thirty minutes. Masako had managed to cross a wide and dangerous intersection that was notorious for automobile accidents and found her way along the busy street. It was as if a guardian angel had walked with her. Although the family had heard about kidnappings for ransom or worse, they thanked God that she had returned home safely. After this event, Tamiko's younger sister, Mitsue, came to babysit Masako until Mitsue left the family to marry. She not only gave her all to care for Masako's well being, but also helped with household chores. Without her help, Tamiko couldn't have continued to do any work.

Another Business Lost

After Mitsuji finally earned enough money to buy the store's title, more trouble arose when the landlord told him that someone was interested in buying the store at a much higher price than Mitsuji had bid. Because the bidder was the landlord's friend, Mitsuji was not given a chance to make another offer. The members of the mall association encouraged him not to give up, but the landlord harassed and intimidated him daily by sitting in front of the store, so Mitsuji finally gave in and moved out. He cried at losing such a successful business, which had not even lasted a year. Many of the shop owners in the mall sympathized with him.

The landlord paid Mitsuji 500,000 yen to move out. (A college graduate's starting annual salary as a banker was about 180,000 yen at the time.) Mitsuji could have fought, but he gave up, went home with the mochi machine, and opened the same business at the original store in front of the shrine. However, the location was not ideal for the mochi store, which ended in failure. Mitsuji couldn't understand why he had seen so much bad luck; despite his good ideas and hard work, his family seemed to be on a constant cycle of rising and falling. Now he had to think of a new business again.

Tamiko's younger sister Mitsue (right) and Masako: Mitsue moved in with Tamiko's family shortly after Masako went missing, 1952.

Hitting Rock Bottom

Since Mitsuji had made some money from the trading business before, he decided to open a mutual investment office where he could trade in specialty commodity stocks, such as red beans, called "red diamonds," a risky investment.

His clients deposited their funds into his company, which added to Tamiko's concern. One of his trusted business associates convinced him to act as guarantor for a loan, and when the man disappeared, Mitsuji was left to repay the loan. This event haunted him for the rest of his life.

When the market dropped sharply, Tamiko knew they were facing grave consequences, and she was sick with worry every day. Eventually, the market crashed. Mitsuji and Tamiko made an immediate payment to the stockbrokers, leaving the family with 14 yen, the equivalent of about 60 cents today. As things spiraled downward, they faced property seizure over tax debts. Facing bankruptcy, Mitsuji lost everything, including his clients' funds.

Tamiko didn't know how to dig her family out of this miserable reality. The more they tried to get out, the deeper they sank. They didn't even have the will to open the windows to see the light, so they remained inside the dark house.

Once the family hit rock bottom, it seemed that there was nothing to hope for. Tamiko couldn't stay at home because each time the phone rang, she worried it was one of the bill collectors. She often stayed at their church until her oldest son came to pick her up after school. As a result of the ongoing stress, the family experienced a host of illnesses; both Tamiko and Mitsuji suffered severe depression, Mitsuji had problems with his vision to the point at which he couldn't see the shrine across from his house, and a few of their children suffered from a contagious eye infection.

During this period, Tamiko was afraid to fall asleep because her depressed husband was thinking of ending his life and the lives of the rest of his family. The oldest son, Yoshimi, was about twelve years old when he overheard Mitsuji tell Tamiko that he was considering throwing them over the Kobe dock near the house because he worried about leaving them after he was gone. When he heard that, Yoshimi yelled, "If you ever do that, I will make sure to survive!" As a precaution, Yoshimi took his siblings to the beach to teach them how to swim, as if he were reliving Tamiko's experience of looking after four younger siblings at an early age. Tamiko was surprised at how fast Yoshimi grew up after his father's failures.

Tamiko went to the ward office for food stamps for her family but was refused and told to get help from Mitsuji's and Tamiko's siblings. Feeling ashamed, they did not ask for help from anyone, but someone found out about their struggles, and the news quickly spread among family and friends who lived in the neighboring cities.

Overwhelming support came to rescue them: Mitsuji's siblings delivered food and pooled their money, while one of his wartime friends, an eye doctor, treated Mitsuji and their children's eye infections, and another wartime friend, a rice shop owner, delivered rice to them every week, saying, "Pay whenever you can; no rush! You need to eat now."

After Tamiko's family—Hiroyuki, Tamiko's siblings—heard about her problems, they took care of her two older children in their hometown during the school break. Mitsuji was encouraged to live again and looked forward to returning everyone's kindness as soon as possible. As he regained his health, his confidence began to rebuild.

Through the experience of financial ruin, Mitsuji realized how many people were in the same situation. He was fortunate to have received such widespread support and felt humbled by their siblings and friends' generosity. If the rescue hadn't arrived on time, he might have chosen to end his own and his family's lives.

The family received full support for about three months until Mitsuji's mood and health recovered, and he was able to stand up to the reality that faced him.

One of Mitsuji's friends offered him a job managing and selling daily commodities, and he began earning some income. During his spare time, Mitsuji did some carpentry work to return favors, little by little, to the people who had saved his family. Despite these positive signs, Tamiko knew it would be a long way to recovery.

Always pursuing his interests, Mitsuji tried to invent new machines, but he had neither the money nor the drawing skill for a patent. One day, he met Mr. Hikichi, an inventor and draftsman, who was also poor and didn't have a steady place to live. Mitsuji invited the man to live with the family so he could help with his invention. However, the man had a strange habit of eating uncooked, dried tofu called *koya dofu* that made Mitsuji uncomfortable. (*Koya dofu* comes in two-inch freeze-dried blocks, which must be soaked in water before cooking. Eating the dry blocks was unheard of, and created a powdery mess.) Tamiko assumed that Mr. Hikichi's behavior brought back unpleasant memories of Mitsuji's wartime meals. Mitsuji's desire to invent a machine was eclipsed by the awkwardness he felt around this man, so he asked the man to leave. After this episode, he gave up inventing machines and stopped inviting strangers into his home.

Still, Mitsuji's generosity remained. Despite having barely enough food for his own family, he didn't ignore the homeless families in the neighborhood and often shared the pickled plums, called *umeboshi* that he made.

Tamiko wondered whether Mitsuji's endless kindness to others might be the reason they had received such amazing support when the family was drowning.

Yoshimi's middle school graduation:
He received the highest achievement award and a prize for
three years of full attendance. Tamiko also received an
encouragement award, 1956.

Finally, the Light Shines in the House

Good news came from one of Mitsuji's relatives, who was helping out Mr. Tsuneoka, a congressman whom Mitsuji and Tamiko supported. Mr. Tsuneoka wanted to rent Mitsuji's empty store for an upcoming campaign, as it was strategically placed near the train station and in front of a famous shrine. Mitsuji and Tamiko rejoiced in the news, feeling honored and excited that the well-known congressman wanted to use their place for his reelection. They decided to allow him to use it free of charge, even though they could have charged a handsome fee for a campaign office. More importantly, they had been hoping for a reason to open the front space, as with the front door closed, the living area in the back remained dark, creating a depressing atmosphere. They were happy and felt that this opportunity was like a rescue boat.

When the election office was set to open, many people began visiting the office, and the house became lively again. The children were excited by meeting so many energetic staff members, and the campaign shined light onto the family and gave them hope in their dark place. They received the kind of joy that couldn't have been bought by money alone.

When Mr. Tsuneoka was reelected, he surprised Tamiko with an expensive kimono set and a gift of 10,000 yen. Mitsuji started thinking about opening a new business with this gift money, determined to make it this time.

Tamiko's family lived in front of Minatogawa shrine. The gate of which is seen behind the family's first car. Mitsuji could park in the open space once their neighbor moved out of the urban project.

The Makeshift Store

Long before the bankruptcy, Mitsuji had acquired a small rental apartment, which was located near the Kawasaki Heavy Industry shipyard in Kobe City. A large dormitory for the shipyard workers stood across the street. It was under Tamiko's brother Saburo's management because of the bankruptcy, but Mitsuji had access to use the property.

Mitsuji went to a nearby wholesale market to salvage wood from discarded crates that had been used to ship apples and other fruits and then spent 7,000 yen for building material and equipment. During their school break, the two older sons, Yoshimi and Yukio, helped finish building a makeshift store that was detached from the apartment. Mitsuji used the remaining 3,000 yen to purchase start-up goods from the wholesale market. The new business opened in August 1954, selling ready-to-eat foods like sweets, cooked vegetables, cut fruits, and much more.

There were more than three hundred illegal houses around the makeshift shop. At that time, the city's urban project to modernize the shattered postwar city was underway, so Mitsuji was ordered to vacate just two months after he opened the store. The city government expressed no mercy, and a large truck with demolition tools was dispatched to his store. Naturally, no one listened to anyone. The workers shouted, "We are here to take it down! Get away!" Setting an example for the other places, the workers demolished his store first because it was the most popular one in the neighborhood and then left the site quickly. Tamiko understood that it was their job to do that.

One of the tenants who lived in the apartment next to the demolished shop watched the demolition in horror and felt sympathy for Mitsuji. The tenants offered to move out so he could build a store attached to the apartment that would be safer and more stable.

Mitsuji knew that he would have to move from the area sooner or later because of the urban project, but he decided to take a chance on building a second convenience store on the same site as the demolished one until the urban project began in full force.

To everyone's surprise, the business was a success. About three hundred shipyard workers living in the dormitory were happy to hang out and socialize at the shop after work until late at night.

Mitsuji installed a new TV, which was a luxury item that few people could own. The shop became their family room, so he expanded the store to accommodate more people, and it became the neighborhood's free-TV theater.

His business prospered and all of his family worked at the store. Sometimes they sold more than sixty watermelons in a day, so many that they eventually warped many of the large knives that they used to cut them. Yoshimi took his younger siblings home early and cared for their schooling while Mitsuji and Tamiko often worked until three in the morning. Sometimes, when they were about to close the shop, the night-shift workers came back, so many nights they couldn't close the store at all. They were exhausted but happy.

Mitsuji managed the store for fifteen years, which was much longer than everyone thought they could stay. Amazingly, the city officials didn't interfere with them.

In 1967 Mitsuji was offered a large sum to move from the land where the family lived to make way for the urban development. He purchased a larger plot of land with the money and built a new house on it.

Above: The make shift store attached to the apartment located in front of the shipyard workers' dormitory, Mitsuji (right) and Masako, 1958.

Below: Tamiko (sitting) with her five children and her niece (bottom left).

Epilogue

Hiroyuki's Passing in 1966

Tamiko's father, Hiroyuki, didn't remarry after his wife's death. He spent his last thirty-six years devoted to ministry work at his church, which he established in his hometown, as he had pledged to do when Saburo became blind. He died peacefully in his sleep at the age of seventy-two.

November 1972

Despite the ups and downs in his family's life, Yoshimi graduated from Osaka University in Japan and was later given a full scholarship to study at Flinders University in Australia, where he received his PhD in physical sciences. Although Tamiko's schooling was cut short by her mother's sudden death, her dream of an education was fulfilled by her son's achievements.

October 1976

Mitsuji paid off all his debt before he died at the age of sixty-eight. It was as if he lifted his family's rocky life with him to heaven. Tamiko and his five children blessed his life, which gave them many valuable life lessons for which to be thankful.

1991

A few years after Tamiko returned home from living in the United States with Masako's family, two of Tamiko's neighbors' houses burned. One of the fires, which burned her neighbor's house to the ground, was only about four yards away from Tamiko's house. Miraculously, her house survived with only minor smoke damage. Tamiko wondered whether Mitsuji's spirit had saved her house.

January 17, 1995

Tamiko woke early in the morning and found herself sitting on her bed with a roaring sound in her ears. A massive earthquake had hit Kobe City, but Tamiko didn't realize it until one of her tenants from upstairs rushed down, shouting, "Earthquake!" Struggling to get Tamiko out of her apartment, the tenant yanked the back door open while Tamiko looked for her footwear in the dark. Minutes later, they managed to get outside.

On the way to the park in the neighborhood, they smelled gas leaking from the damaged houses. Many people were assembled at the park, and Tamiko overheard people warning each other not to smoke because of the risk of an explosion. She had never been so frightened.

As hours passed, members from the self-defense forces helped them to the evacuation site, where everyone was fed and sheltered. Fortunately, Tamiko's children found her there, and she stayed at her daughter's house for three weeks while the utility lines were repaired.

Returning home, she was relieved to find her concrete building standing firmly, although it was leaning slightly. Many of the surrounding wooden houses had been completely flattened. Months later the city officials condemned the front half of Tamiko's building. (Mitsuji had built two separate structures; the front half was for the family to live in, and the other half was for apartments to rent.) Fortunately, the back half could be renovated. Before the front half of the building was demolished, Tamiko's third son, Kaoru, who was good at carpentry work, built a smaller apartment for her at the same address, where she currently lives.

April 29, 2008

Tamiko's second eldest son, Yukio, was presented a Yellow Ribbon Medal of Honor by Prime Minister Fukuda. This medal is given to a civilian who has contributed his or her time and effort to public service for more than thirty years. It was a great honor, and all the recipients were invited to visit the royal palace to meet Emperor Akihito.

April 8, 2010

Tamiko's brother Saburo died peacefully at the age of eighty-one, survived by his wife, two children, and six grandchildren. He had a happy, healthy, normal life, despite his early weakness and the scare of permanent blindness. Tamiko misses the time when he visited her during the two years before he died. He often cooked her favorite rice meal and was pleased when she said, "It's delicious. Thank you."

2013

Although Tamiko's children endured Mitsuji's string of failures in his businesses, none of them experienced such difficulties as adults, and all of them maintain comfortable lives. Tamiko has been able to manage living by herself well into her nineties. She assumes that these survival skills gradually grew from the experience of overcoming many hardships. She has eleven grandchildren and five great-grandchildren, and the family is still growing.

Attending Tamiko's sister, Fujiko's wedding, circa 1951.
In the white circles on this ceremonial kimono are the family crests.

Mitsuji's family and his relatives: Mitsuji (top right), his sister, Mrs. Kawamura and her children (bottom right next to their parents.), circa 1933.

Tamiko's family:
Left to right, Father Hiroyuki, brother Saburo, Aunt Sasaki, sister Mitsue, cousin Ms.Umemoto, sister Fujiko, brother Makoto, circa 1940.

(Photo courtesy of Tamiko's nephew Masanori)

Tamiko's daughter, Keiko's wedding day: Left to right, Masako, Tamiko (standing), Kaoru, and Keiko (in bridal kimono), 1971.

The last family gathering with Tamiko's husband:
Top row: Left to right, Yoshimi, Masako, Kaoru, Keiko's husband, Yoshio;
Keiko and their 2 sons, Kenji and Takahiro; Tamiko (kneeling).
Middle row: Yoshimi's wife, Sachiko; Tamiko's sister-in-law, Matsu;
Mitsuji, Yukio and his wife, Chizuru.
Bottom row: Yoshimi's 2 daughters, Junko and Yuhko;
Yukio's 2 children, Hiroko and Kohji, 1976.

Tamiko's first visit to the U.S: Holding grandson, Yosef who is wearing a Japanese ceremonial kimono for newborns, previously worn by her sons, 1980.

The 2nd visit: One of Tamiko's daily enjoyments was walking with her grandchildren, Yosef and Leah, 1984.

The 3rd visit:
Playing "tea time"
with Leah in the yard,
1987.

Playing cards with Leah, while Yosef enjoys reading a comic book.

 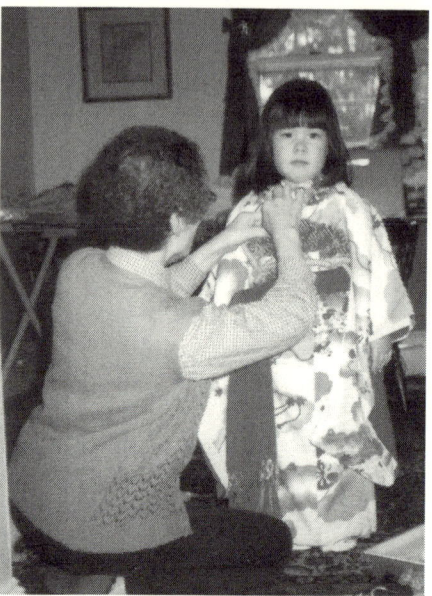

Dressing Leah in a kimono for the Japanese holiday called Hinamatsuri, a doll festival for girls on March 3, 1988.

Above: Right to left, Tamiko, Leah, Jay (Masako's husband), and family guests at Masako's relatives' Passover Seder, April 1988.

Below: Tamiko's handwritten memoir, 1988.

*Tamiko's father, Hiroyuki's 30th memorial service was
held at the church that he established, 1996.*

*Tamiko's siblings:
Left to right, Makoto, Mitsue, Tamiko Fujiko, Saburo, 1996.*

(Photo courtesy of Tamiko's nephew Masanori)

Tamiko, 2004.

(Photographed by Leah)

Coauthor

Masako Glushien is Tamiko's youngest child. She grew up in Kobe
City, Japan, and spent a year in Australia learning English with the
help of her host families. Prior to coming to America, she worked
in Osaka, Japan, as a children's clothing designer. She lives with her
husband in Massachusetts.